HISTORIC MAPS AND VIEWS OF
LONDON

George Sinclair

BLACK DOG
& LEVENTHAL
PUBLISHERS
NEW YORK

Published by
Black Dog & Leventhal Publishers, Inc.
151 West 19th Street
New York, NY 10011

Distributed by
Workman Publishing Company
225 Varick Street
New York, NY 10014

Image credits:
© **Alfred Daniels** 23
© **akg-images** 7; © British Library, 20
Art Resource, NY © HIP 1, 9; © The Stapleton Collection 14
Author's Private Collection 18
The Bridgeman Art Library © Private Collection/The Stapleton Collection 2; © Guildhall Library, City of London, 5, 10, 21;
© City of Westminster Archive Centre, London, UK, 13; © Private Collection, 19
Corbis © Stapleton Collection 8; © The Gallery Collection 11, 17;© Swim Ink 2, LLC 22
© **Getty Images** 15
© **Max Roberts** 24
© **Museum of London** 3, 4, 6, 12, 16

Manufactured in China

Cover and interior design by Toshiya Masuda

ISBN-13: 978-1-57912-797-8

h g f e d c b a

Library of Congress Cataloging-in-Publication Data available on file.

INTRODUCTION

Maps have existed since the time of the ancient Egyptians. Even Alexander the Great (336–323 BC), whose empire extended as far as India, had mapmakers who accompanied him on his campaigns. The Greek geographer Strabo (born in 63 BC) produced *Geographia*, a collection of seventeen books describing the geographical scope of Europe, Asia, and Africa. The collection comprises his own observations, historical material, and descriptions of places he had seen and people he had met during his travels. A number of later versions of *Geographia* were published until the fourteenth century.

Although many of these books survived, most maps produced during this time did not, and it was not until the fifteenth century that maps really began to be preserved. Although London was established by the Romans 2,000 years ago, very few original maps or views of the city existed before 1500. Much of the city during this period was contained within an area measuring one mile by one mile, nearly 720 acres of land, with many people living outside the city walls in small villages and farming communities.

Since the sixteenth century, due to the pressure of economic conditions, social change, technological advancements, the domination of Europe through its supremacy of the oceans, the colonization of foreign lands, and the political power of the city of London over the rest of Great Britain, London has outgrown its boundaries time and time again. Villages and settlements were absorbed into the capital to eventually form the home counties and, subsequently, the boroughs of Greater London, stretching some fifteen to twenty miles from the center of the city. For four hundred years, people have been asking the same questions, which remain of special urgency today: how big is London, and where does London stop?

These and other similar questions have been answered, in part, by the map. In the early days, it was Dutch and German engravers, with their engraving and printing expertise, who published maps of London. The first known full-scale map of London was produced around 1550 by a cartographer thought to be Anthony van den Wyngaerde. Unfortunately only a fragment exists of a version engraved on copperplate and a woodcut derivative.

The first full map of London to survive is an engraving by Frans Hogenberg that was published in 1572 (Map 2). This map depicts London just before the reign of Queen Elizabeth I, at a time when the City of London had a population of about 75,000.

Although a number of panoramic drawings and views of London were produced in the first half of the seventeenth century, it was the Great Fire of London in 1666 that provided the next great impetus to create maps, plans, and views of the city. The fire raged for five days, destroying 13,000 houses and 89 churches (including St. Paul's Cathedral), and covered an area of 420 acres. Eighty percent of the City of London was destroyed and 80,000 people were evacuated.

During the reconstruction of the city, the roads were widened and brick buildings were erected (prior to the fire, many of the houses and public buildings were constructed of highly flammable wood and tar). Of course, new maps and plans had to be drawn as the rebuilding of London continued over many years under the direction of the head of the Commission for the Rebuilding of London, Sir Christopher Wren.

During the early part of the eighteenth century, very few maps of the city were produced, and those that were were reprints or new editions of old maps or were imported from Holland, where most of the printing in Europe was being done at that time. However, in 1712, a duty of 30 percent was imposed on imported maps, and thereafter the production of London maps returned gradually to London publishers. The Rocque family, immigrants from France, embarked on an ambitious plan to survey the entire City of London. The map took nine years to complete, was divided into squares and numbered for reference, and included an index of the streets. It was published in 1746 and became the standard format for future city maps.

During the nineteenth century, many new elegant houses and public buildings were erected, first by the Georgians and continuing through the Regency period and the era of Queen Victoria, as were new roads, canals, tramways, and railways. The ever-changing face of London resulted, again, in the need for new maps and plans for the citizens and the many visitors to the city.

Detailed maps were produced for the Metropolitan Police, formed in 1829, covering the city to the outskirts and eventually including all parishes within fifteen miles of the capital (the area that became known as Greater London). Many maps detailing the sewers and tunnels of the city, as well as the waterworks, waterways (canals), and rivers, were drawn by city authorities. Maps were also produced to identify the boroughs of London—some even showed the political leanings or wealth of the city.

Transportation became a key factor in the growth of London and, as such, the need for transport maps grew steadily. Route maps of the railway, steam tramways, and horse-drawn buses became essential once these services were introduced in Victorian London, and again for the Electric Railways (now the Underground or "Tube") when they were introduced in 1870.

London and its environment has always been of great interest to engravers and publishers and has been the fascination of historians, illustrators, and painters who either lived in the capital or were visitors to this famous city. Oil paintings came into vogue in the sixteenth century, when the royal and wealthy families commissioned portraits of their relatives and likenesses of their estates to hang on their walls, as well as depictions of the great buildings of London and other historic places of recognition.

Many of the drawings, engravings, and lithographs on the history of London were produced for books and for magazines and newspapers of the day (such as the *Illustrated London News, The Times of London,* and *Vanity Fair*). Paintings and drawings of London also served to emphasize that the city had become the established political center of England because of its financial and commercial power. The Thames River was a symbol of that power, and there are several images in this collection that depict the river as a thriving hub of business through its dockyards, wharfs, barges, markets, and manufacturing industry.

Whereas the Great Fire of London was the catalyst for the redevelopment and growth of medieval London, it was the devastation caused during World War II that was ultimately responsible for the current shape and architecture of modern London. Between 1940 and 1941, London was heavily bombed by the German air force in an effort to cripple the city's financial industry, transport services, shipping channels, and the movement of goods in and out of the city. Much of the center of London was destroyed and had to be rebuilt. The contemporary painting by Alfred Daniels, "Lambeth Palace and the House of Commons" (Map 23), captures London as it looks today, the Thames now serene and serving London mainly as a tourist attraction.

These days the invention of commercial photography has taken over as the popular format for capturing views of the city. Most modern maps of London are practical guides for getting people from one part of town to another or for traveling through the city to specific destinations, and visitors to London are easily recognizable as they pore over printed maps of the city or the Underground.

A FROST FAIR ON THE THAMES AT TEMPLE STAIRS.

OIL ON CANVAS BY ABRAHAM HONDIUS, C. 1684.

THE GREAT FIRE OF LONDON, 1666.

OIL ON WOOD, DUTCH SCHOOL, C. 1666, ARTIST UNKNOWN.

LONDON FROM SOUTHWARK.

OIL ON WOOD, C. 1630, ARTIST UNKNOWN.

THE TOWER OF LONDON.

LONDON'S DOCKLANDS AT WAPPING, LATE EIGHTEENTH CENTURY.

ENGRAVING BY THOMAS & WILLIAM DANIELL, 1803.

BUCKINGHAM PALACE, AT THE TIME OF THE RESIDENCE OF KING GEORGE IV.

Ink and watercolor by Augustus Charles Pugin, 1827.

Her Majesties Royal Palace at Kensington

To Her most Serene and most Sacred Majesty, Anne by y.ᵉ Grace of God QUEEN of Great Britain France & Ireland &c.

SURVEY OF THE ROYAL PALACE OF KENSINGTON FOR HER MAJESTY, ANNE,
QUEEN OF GREAT BRITAIN, FRANCE, AND IRELAND (1702–1714).

ENGRAVING BY JOHANNES KIP, 1730 (AFTER A LEONARD KNYFF ENGRAVING).

THE CRYSTAL PALACE.

LITHOGRAPH OF THE GREAT EXHIBITION, 1851.

WESTMINSTER BRIDGE, THE HOUSES OF PARLIAMENT, AND WESTMINSTER ABBEY.

Oil on canvas, by John McVicar Anderson, 1872.

A Tribute to Sir Christopher Wren.

The Pool of London during the Docklands Air Raids.

Painting by Charles Pears, 1940.

BRITAIN

LONDON

The House of Commons and the House of Lords, together with such adjuncts as Big Ben and historic Westminster Hall, are collectively known as The Palace of Westminster. The present building dates from 1859, its predecessor having been destroyed by fire in 1834; the House of Commons dates from 1950, the former Chamber having been totally destroyed during a bombing attack on 10 May, 1941. Representative government began in Westminster Hall in 1265.

PUBLISHED BY THE BRITISH TRAVEL AND HOLIDAYS ASSOCIATION AND PRINTED IN GREAT BRITAIN BY W. S. COWELL, LTD., AT THE BUTTER MARKET, IPSWICH 54/17/4

BY GEORGE AYLING, M.R.S.T., S.M.A.

The Palace of Westminster and the River Thames.

Poster of London by George Ayling, 1954.

LAMBETH PALACE AND THE HOUSE OF COMMONS.

ACRYLIC PAINTING BY ALFRED DANIELS, RBA, RWS, ARCA, 1978.

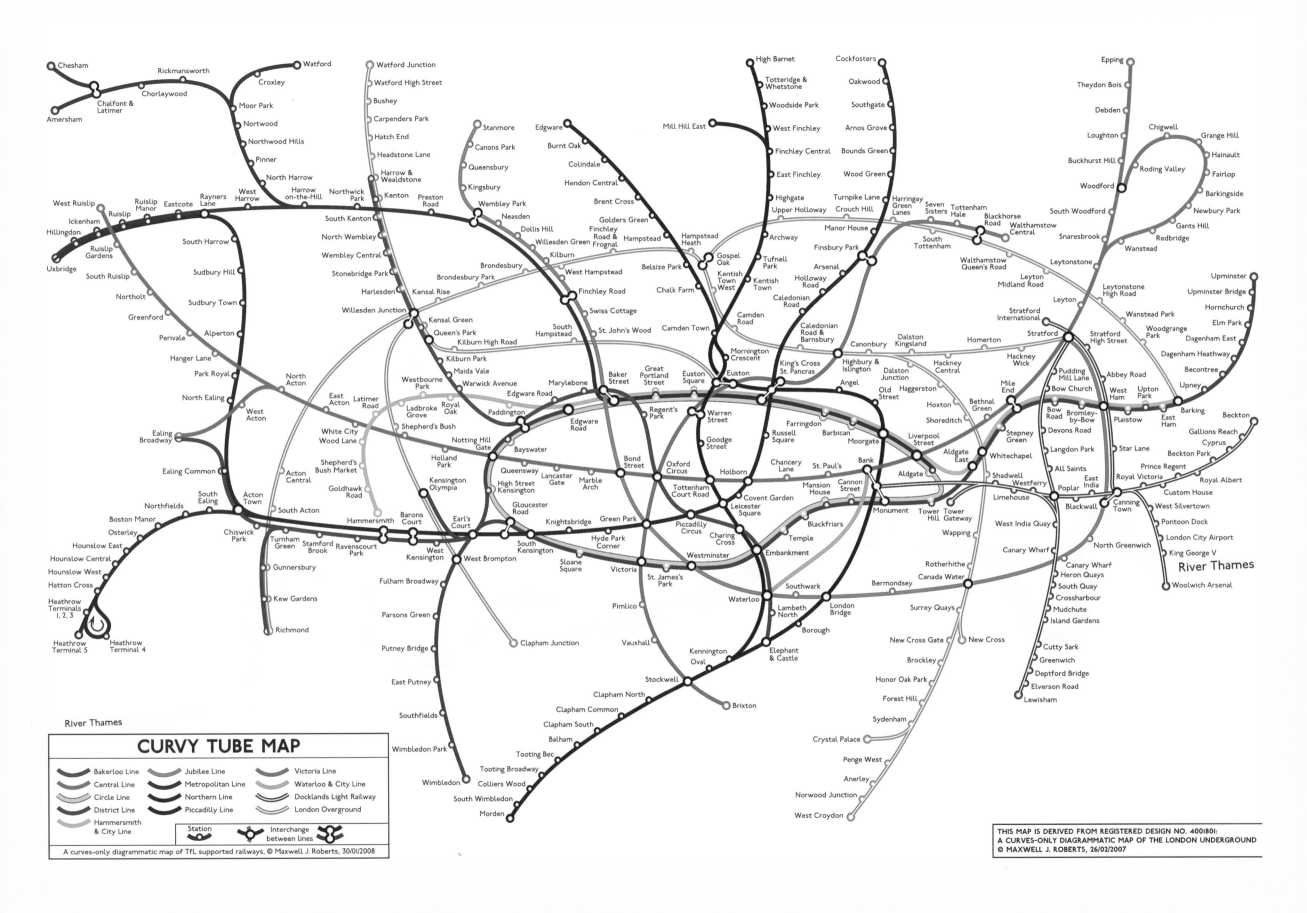

CURVY TUBE MAP

River Thames

Bakerloo Line	Jubilee Line	Victoria Line
Central Line	Metropolitan Line	Waterloo & City Line
Circle Line	Northern Line	Docklands Light Railway
District Line	Piccadilly Line	London Overground
Hammersmith & City Line		

Station   Interchange between lines

A curves-only diagrammatic map of TfL supported railways, © Maxwell J. Roberts, 30/01/2008

THIS MAP IS DERIVED FROM REGISTERED DESIGN NO. 400180I:
A CURVES-ONLY DIAGRAMMATIC MAP OF THE LONDON UNDERGROUND
© MAXWELL J. ROBERTS, 26/02/2007

CURVY MAP OF THE LONDON UNDERGROUND (TUBE) AND DOCKLANDS LIGHT RAILWAY.

ILLUSTRATION BY MAXWELL J. ROBERTS, 2005 (AFTER BECK'S LONDON UNDERGROUND MAPS).

CHARLES D'ORLÉANS IN THE TOWER OF LONDON.

THE EARLIEST KNOWN PAINTING OF LONDON, C. 1500, ARTIST UNKNOWN.

This early-sixteenth-century miniature painting shows an original view of London with the White Tower (now part of the Tower of London), London Bridge, and the City of London (including St. Paul's Cathedral) as they appeared around 1500. This painting, done in England for Henry VII or his son Prince Arthur, in the Flemish style, is considered to be one of the earliest known paintings of London and was painted as the decorative frontispiece to a volume of poems composed by the Duke of Orléans. The Duke, joint commander of the French forces at the Battle of Agincourt, was taken prisoner on the battlefield and held in London for twenty-five years.

He is shown in the upper window of the White Tower, where he is being held for a ransom of 300,000 crowns; again in the lower gallery, writing to his brother in 1440 to give him news of his pending return; being greeted upon his release; and finally, riding away on horseback through the drawbridge.

In the background is the Old London Bridge, and the City of London just beyond.

MAP OF MID-TUDOR LONDON.

ENGRAVED BY FRANS HOGENBERG, BASED ON A DRAWING BY GEORGE HOEFNAGEL. PUBLISHED IN *CIVITAS ORBIS TERRARUM* BY BRAUN AND HOGENBERG, 1572.

This engraved map is assumed to be the work of Frans Hogenberg and was probably based on a drawing by George Hoefnagel. It shows London in the 1550s just before the reign of Elizabeth I, which began in 1558. London, barely one square mile, is bounded by green fields and the river. At this time, the City of London had a population of about 75,000, with another 150,000 people living outside the medieval walls. The city walls were built on the original Roman foundations. Westminster Abbey is to the west, around the river bend, connected to the city by the main road through Whitehall, Charing Cross, Covent Garden, and across Fleet River. To the east of the city lies the White Tower, now part of the Tower of London. South of the river lies Southwark, a mainly rural area with a small village to the east and the Archbishop of Canterbury's palace at Lambeth Marshes to the west. Old London Bridge is depicted with houses and shops built upon it. It was the only bridge to span the Thames River in London until 1750, when Westminster Bridge was opened.

A FROST FAIR ON THE THAMES AT TEMPLE STAIRS.

OIL ON CANVAS BY ABRAHAM HONDIUS, C. 1684.

Due to the narrow arches and breakwaters of the Old London Bridge, the Thames River froze over on a number of occasions and paralyzed river traffic. In 1684, the cold weather froze the river upstream from the bridge and street fairs were created by building tents on the ice between Temple Stairs (at the Strand) and the South Bank. Various sporting events were held, including bull baiting (dog fighting), bear baiting (men are invited to fight bears who have been whipped into a frenzy), and fox hunting, as well as games and activities such as dancing, ox roasting, football, ninepins, and horse sledding. The horses' hooves were either spiked or wrapped in linen cloth to give them a grip on the ice. Even King Charles II and the royal family visited the Frost Fair. The view depicts the king's visit, which was celebrated with the firing of three cannons by the Household Cavalry—seen here quite small and surrounded by hundreds of people. The freeze lasted from mid-December to mid-February.

Records reveal that the Thames froze twenty-three times beginning in 1309, and Frost Fairs were recorded in 1677, 1684, 1715, 1739, 1789, and 1814. The last Frost Fair was held in 1831, before the New London Bridge was opened.

THE GREAT FIRE OF LONDON, 1666.

OIL ON WOOD, DUTCH SCHOOL, C. 1666, ARTIST UNKNOWN.

The Great Fire of London broke out in the early morning of September 2, 1666, on Pudding Lane in a bakeshop that catered to Charles II. The city was just recovering from yet another plague, and the dead were still being buried in mass graves.

The fire, fanned by winds and kindled by pitch-coated wooden buildings, burned westward and across London Bridge and consumed 80 percent of the City of London (some 430 acres), destroying 13,000 houses, 89 churches, including St. Paul's Cathedral, and 52 guildhalls.

Remarkably, only ten known deaths were recorded as a result of the fire, which raged for nearly five days. Eighty thousand people were evacuated (the total population at that time was four hundred thousand) and some twenty thousand choose not to return to the city. Plague, however, was eradicated due to the mass death of rats. Fire insurance became popular.

The view shows St. Paul's Cathedral in the center of the fire and Old London Bridge to the left. The Tower of London is shown clearly to the right of the painting.

AFTER THE GREAT FIRE OF LONDON.

COLORED ENGRAVING BY MARCUS WILLEMSZ DOORNIK DEPICTING THE FIRE, THE AREA DESTROYED BY THE FIRE, AND THE PROPOSED PLANS FOR REBUILDING THE CITY, C. 1675.

After the Great Fire of London in 1666, a plan was drawn up to provide the city with wider streets and brick buildings. Sir Christopher Wren was commissioned to design and supervise the construction of fifty-one new churches, including the reconstruction of St. Paul's Cathedral, which was destroyed in the fire. In 1676, another fire south of the Thames River destroyed six hundred houses. These two fires created an opportunity to radically remake the city and changed the face of London forever. The six commissioners appointed to redesign the city drew up the most comprehensive town-planning legislation ever seen in England.

Rebuilding continued in spite of the wars with the Dutch, the Monmouth Rebellion, and the revolution of 1688. By 1671, nine thousand brick buildings had been erected. St. Paul's Cathedral was rebuilt between 1675 and 1711 and was considered the crowning glory of Wren's remarkable body of work.

Many of the residents who fled the fires did not return to the city.

LONDON FROM SOUTHWARK.

OIL ON WOOD, C. 1630, ARTIST UNKNOWN.

This view shows London as seen from the south side of the Thames River as it appeared in 1630, before the Great Fire of London. In the foreground are the playhouses (the Globe, the Rose, the Hope, and the Swan) and the Church of St. Mary Overy (later to become Southwark Cathedral).

The wooden London Bridge is overcrowded with houses and shops and Thomas à Becket Chapel. In the center of the bridge is a drawbridge, which would have allowed tall sailing ships and galleons to pass through. Also on the bridge is Nonsuch House, thought to be the residence of the lord mayor of London.

Note the heads of executed convicts on poles atop the building at the southern end of the bridge. They were left there to deter the population from criminal acts.

St. Paul's Cathedral dominates the city, much of which was to be subsequently destroyed by the Great Fire. The Tower of London is shown to the right of the panoramic view.

PANORAMIC VIEW OF LONDON.

COPPER ENGRAVING BY MARTIN ENGELBRECHT, C. 1750.

This panorama of churches represents many of those that were rebuilt by Sir Christopher Wren, or under his supervision, after the Great Fire of London in 1666, which destroyed or badly damaged eighty-nine churches, including St. Paul's Cathedral. As surveyor general, Wren was responsible for rebuilding many of those churches, the best known of which were St. Stephen at Walbrook, St. Mary on Abchurch Lane, St. Bride on Fleet Street, St. Mary-le-Bow, and of course, St. Paul's.

In the fifty-seven years between the Great Fire and his death, Wren's rate of rebuilding was astonishing; he established his own style of architecture, which greatly influenced other architects. He was also responsible for the design of the Custom House and Royal Hospital Chelsea.

THE TOWER OF LONDON.

ENGRAVING BY CHARLES RIVIERE IN THE STYLE OF ACHILLE-LOUIS MARTINET, C. 1862.

After defeating King Harold in the Battle of Hastings (the Saxon king was mortally wounded when an arrow struck his eye), the Normandy invader, William the Conqueror, was hastily crowned king at Westminster Abbey. He soon thereafter began construction on the Tower of London, starting with the White Tower in 1078. The Tower of London was designed to accommodate the king, the royal family, its household, and the king's treasure. The inner defense walls, made up of twelve towers, were added later by King Henry III (1216–1272). King Edward I (1272–1307) added the outer defenses, including the Traitor's Gate (used to transport criminals who had committed or plotted treason against the king from the Thames River to the Tower of London).

The Tower became the place of imprisonment, torture, and execution. After his brother King Edward IV died suddenly and unexpectedly in 1483, it is reputed that Richard III had his nephew and younger brother murdered in the tower as he was preparing for his own coronation. Elizabeth I ordered the execution of her cousin Mary Queen of Scots at the tower in 1587. Mary had been imprisoned in the tower for years after she was linked to an assassination attempt on Queen Elizabeth in St. James's Park.

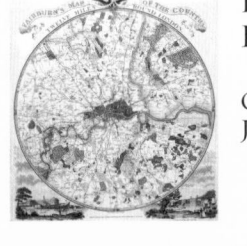

FAIRBURNS MAP OF THE COUNTRY TWELVE MILES ROUND LONDON.

CHART AND MAP ENGRAVED BY E. BOURNE AND PUBLISHED BY JOHN FAIRBURN, AUGUST 1, 1798.

Many of the major roads leading out of London were established by the Roman army connecting Londinium—as the city was known when first settled by the invaders in AD 60—with other major garrisons, such as Verulamium (now Saint Albans), Camulodunum (now Colchester), Durovernum (now Canterbury), and Aquae Sulis (now Bath—the site of the Roman spa baths).

During the Roman occupation of London, many of the Saxons lived outside the city and established villages where farming was the primary occupation.

By the eighteenth century the area around London had grown to a large metropolis of towns and villages that made up the counties of Kent, Essex, Middlesex, Surrey, and London. Travel was by foot, horse, or horse-drawn carriage, and therefore many coaching inns were established along the main roads leading in and out of London.

The view on the bottom left shows Chelsea Hospital, and the view on the right is of Greenwich Hospital.

LONDON'S DOCKLANDS AT WAPPING, LATE EIGHTEENTH CENTURY.

ENGRAVING BY THOMAS & WILLIAM DANIELL, 1803.

England's navy was built under the direction of Elizabeth I, when she became Queen in 1558, as a strong wall and defense against the enemies of England, who at the time consisted mainly of Spain. The rise of the navy led to the establishment of the Royal Dockyards in Deptford and Woolwich, and the many private dockyards that lined the Thames River from the Medway to London Bridge, including the Limehouse and Wapping dockyards. It was during this early period that Sir Francis Drake first sailed around the world in a journey lasting some three years and four months, ending in London in 1581.

It was, however, the merchant or commercial shipping that ushered in the vast network of docklands. For 250 years, commencing with regulations dating from the time of Elizabeth I, every ship coming up the Thames River had to unload all dutiable cargo at the twenty quays, known as the Legal Quays, that were crowded side by side between London Bridge and the Tower of London at Wapping. Legal Quays included the London Docks, built at the beginning of the nineteenth century, and St. Katharine Docks, which was added in 1828.

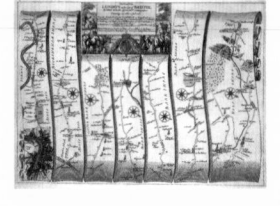

THE ROAD FROM LONDON WEST TO THE CITY OF BRISTOL.

MAP BY JOHN OGILBY, 1675.

John Ogilby was His Majesty's (Charles II) cartographer and was responsible for a number of the maps of the City of London. He also created the first encyclopedia of maps of England.

The road to Bristol was first established by Roman soldiers for their movements and to ferry supplies. The Romans were practical road engineers and therefore built roads that were raised and cambered so the rain would run off. The road was essential because it connected the City of London not only to the spas in Bath, but also to the seaport of Bristol for access to Wales and Ireland.

BUCKINGHAM PALACE, AT THE TIME OF THE RESIDENCE OF KING GEORGE IV.

INK AND WATERCOLOR BY AUGUSTUS CHARLES PUGIN, 1827.

Compared to other royal palaces, Buckingham Palace is not that old. It was built as a private residence in 1702 for the Duke of Buckingham, the illegitimate son of King James II. It has been much altered and remodeled over the years, beginning with George III in 1762. In 1820, George IV hired the famous architect John Nash (responsible also for the Nash terraced houses in Regent's Park and the Royal Pavilion in Brighton) to rebuild the palace with a three-sided court open to the east, facing the Mall and Trafalgar Square. In 1830, the newly married Queen Victoria appointed the architect Edward Blore to enclose the courtyard.

Buckingham Palace is flanked by St. James's Park and Marlborough House (the former home of Queen Elizabeth II's grandmother), Clarence House (the former home of the Queen Mother), St. James's Palace (the London home of Price Charles), Lancaster House, and Green Park. The palace is approached along the Mall as you pass under Admiralty Arch from Trafalgar Square.

Buckingham Palace is the London home of Queen Elizabeth II and her family when she is not staying at Windsor Castle, Sandringham Estate, or Balmoral Castle.

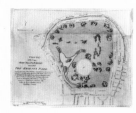

PLAN OF REGENT'S PARK, 1822.

DRAWN BY J BRIGGS AND PRINTED BY BOOSEY & CO.

Beginning in 1811, the architect John Nash designed and built Piccadilly Circus (originally Regent Circus), Regent Street, Oxford Circus, Portland Place, and finally, Cumberland Terrace and Chester Terrace. Regent Street was the brainchild of the prince regent (the heir to George IV), who envisioned a "Royal Mile," after the magnificent boulevards of Napoleon's Paris. The grand street was to run from his official residence at Carlton House to his summerhouse in the park.

Regent's Park was planned in 1822. The Zoological Gardens (now London Zoo) was added at a later date to replace the Menagerie that was founded in medieval times by King Henry III as a tourist attraction.

During the winter many people skated on the pond in Regent's Park. However, disaster struck in January 1867 when the ice broke and forty-one people drowned as thousands stood helplessly on the banks. New regulations were introduced for London's parks that forbid skating unless the ice was five inches thick. Subsequently, a number of lakes were made very shallow.

SURVEY OF THE ROYAL PALACE OF KENSINGTON FOR HER MAJESTY, ANNE, QUEEN OF GREAT BRITAIN, FRANCE, AND IRELAND (1702–1714).

ENGRAVING BY JOHANNES KIP, 1730 (AFTER A LEONARD KNYFF ENGRAVING).

When William of Orange (a Dutch prince) and Queen Mary (the daughter of King James) ascended to the throne in 1689, William was most unhappy with the royal residence of St. James's Palace. In order to provide a suitable home for the royal family, he commissioned Sir Christopher Wren to significantly enlarge a private house that he had purchased. He had acquired the house, along with twenty-six acres of land in the village of Kensington, from Lord Nottingham for twenty thousand pounds. Unfortunately, Mary died of smallpox in 1694, just four years after Kensington Palace was completed. William died there eight years later after a fall from his horse.

On her succession in 1702, Queen Anne significantly increased the grounds, as is depicted in this view, by adding one hundred acres. The Serpentine Lake (not shown on the survey) was added in 1730 so the royal family could sail pleasure boats.

It is clear from the survey that Queen Anne expanded the palace to be a lavish place. Diana, Princess of Wales, was resident at Kensington Palace until her death in 1997, and her official memorial is located in the park.

THE CRYSTAL PALACE.

LITHOGRAPH OF THE GREAT EXHIBITION, 1851.

Originally built to house the Great Exhibition of the Works of Industry of All Nations in 1851, the Crystal Palace, as it was called, was considered the architectural marvel of its age. The building, constructed of delicate cast iron and covered with three hundred thousand panes of glass, covered a full nineteen acres of Hyde Park. The exhibition galleries totaled nearly two miles and in some places stood over one hundred feet in order to accommodate the tall elm trees displayed inside. The Crystal Palace was built in just four months using nine hundred thousand square feet of glass. Some panes were four feet long and one foot wide. The strength of the building was tested by pulling eight-ton carts filled with cannonballs up and down the galleries, and marching soldiers around the building in close formation. When Queen Victoria opened the exhibition, complete with more than one hundred thousand exhibits, on May 1, 1851, twenty-five thousand people filled the building.

In the five months it was open, the exhibition attracted six million people, equal to one-third of the population.

The Crystal Palace was reerected in South London and remained open for exhibitions and entertainment until it burned to the ground in 1936.

WESTMINSTER BRIDGE, THE HOUSES OF PARLIAMENT, AND WESTMINSTER ABBEY.

OIL ON CANVAS BY JOHN McVICAR ANDERSON, 1872, SIGNED AND DATED.

This moonlit view shows the Houses of Parliament, with their long river frontage, flanked by Victoria Tower on the far side and the Clock Tower (affectionately know as Big Ben and likely named after the commissioner of works at the time). St. Stephen's Hall, once used as one of the Houses of Parliament, is the middle tower. Westminster Bridge, seen in the foreground, is the replacement for the original bridge built in the mid-eighteenth century.

The disastrous fire of 1834 destroyed most of the historic Palace of Westminster, except Westminster Hall. The Gothic design of the new Houses of Parliament was the creation of Augustus Pugin and established a new concept in design among leading architects of the time. The building was completed in 1860.

Westminster Abbey and the early Tudor parish church of St. Margaret's at its rear are shown to the right. Westminster Abbey, built by the Saxons under Edward the Confessor, was completed in 1065 and became the location for the coronation of the kings and queens of England and the burial place for many of its royal and noble subjects.

A TRIBUTE TO SIR CHRISTOPHER WREN.

WATERCOLOR PAINTING BY CHARLES ROBERT COCKERELL, 1870.

Sir Christopher Wren was appointed joint head of a group of six commissioners to redesign the city after the Great Fire of London in 1666. Although his own radical plan for the city was rejected, he still designed and supervised the rebuilding of fifty-one of the eighty-nine new churches, including St. Paul's Cathedral. Although it took twenty-one years to rebuild St. Paul's, the speed with which Wren rebuilt parts of London was remarkable. Most of the churches were rebuilt in sixteen years, beginning in 1670. And 75 percent of the city had been rebuilt within five years.

The view sets out to create a collage of the churches Wren rebuilt and to salute his greatest achievement, St. Paul's Cathedral.

MAP OF LONDON IN COMMEMORATION OF THE GREAT EXHIBITION OF INDUSTRY OF ALL NATIONS, 1851.

ENGRAVING BY JOHN TALLIS & CO, 1851. RELEASED AS A FOLDING MAP OF LONDON.

The Great Exhibition of Industry of All Nations was held in Hyde Park under the glass exhibition building known as the Crystal Palace. Queen Victoria's husband, the prince consort, was president of the event, a show of many different industrial displays with more than one hundred thousand exhibits. Six million people, many from overseas, attended the Great Exhibition.

The idea of this map was to furnish visitors with a folded guide to London as well as a souvenir of the wonderful places and buildings they may have seen while visiting.

The border consists of forty-nine views "of all the Public Buildings and Places of Amusement in the British Metropolis and its suburbs." Such views include theaters, parks, the Zoological Gardens, museums, and other places of entertainment and interest.

EARLY MAP OF THE LONDON UNDERGROUND.

ENGRAVED, C. 1880.

This color lithograph from the late nineteenth century shows the early stages of the London Underground. The world's first underground track opened in London in 1863 as part of the Metropolitan Railway from Paddington to Farringdon Street, near St. Paul's Cathedral, and was used for freight services. The Underground Service was founded in 1870 when the underground system began to be used for passenger services. Electric trains were introduced to replace steam engines, and the term "rush hour" came into being as a result of the heavy use at the beginning of each workday. The Underground became known commonly as the "Tube," after the introduction of the Twopenny Tube Central Line in 1900.

In the early days the Underground routes were marked as overlays on existing maps. Before long, routes were represented on the map as color-coded lines connecting each of the stations, which eliminated extraneous detail. By 1912, the Underground Service was under the control of the Underground Electric Railways Company, and in 1933, the coordination passed to London Transport along with the oversight of buses, coaches, and trams. Today the Underground carries 3 million passengers every weekday, has 255 miles of subway lines, and connects more than 360 stations.

London Transport and the British government installed floodgates at major stations at the beginning of World War II as emergency antiflooding measures were taken on the north side of the Thames River. The stations and tunnels were used as bomb shelters during World War II. It was estimated that 175,000 people took nightly cover in the deep subterranean tube stations.

THE WONDERGROUND MAP OF LONDON TOWN.

COLOR PRINT OF THE OVERGROUND MAP OF LONDON. DRAWING BY MACDONALD GILL, C. 1915.

This tourist map showing the attractions of the city and the location of the Underground stations provided direction for travelers on trams, electric trains (the Underground), and motor-driven buses. The map covers the eight boroughs that made up the center of London at the beginning of the twentieth century.

With more and more citizens commuting from the suburbs to the city during this period, there was rapid growth in the use of public transportation. Adding to this growth was also a great need for the transport of people displaced by enemy bombing during World War I.

THE POOL OF LONDON DURING THE DOCKLANDS AIR RAIDS.

PAINTING BY CHARLES PEARS, 1940.

During World War II, England, and London in particular, was bombed heavily by the German air forces in 1940 and 1941, the period known as the "Blitz." In 1944, enemy V-1 and V-2 rockets sent from continental Europe and across the English Channel further destroyed vast areas of London.

The majority of the bombing was concentrated in the City (the financial center of London) and in the East End of London, where the docklands were situated, so as to disrupt business, shipping, cross-river links, and the movement of armament supplies. In this stark view, from 1941, the searchlight beams meet above Tower Bridge in search of enemy aircraft, with the East End of London ablaze in the background. An estimated 43,000 civilians were killed during the Blitz.

THE PALACE OF WESTMINSTER AND THE RIVER THAMES.

POSTER OF LONDON BY GEORGE AYLING, 1954.

This poster depicts the House of Commons and the House of Lords, which together with Big Ben, St. Stephen's Church, Westminster Hall, and Victoria Tower are collectively known as the Palace of Westminster. Representative government began in Westminster Hall in 1265 under kings Henry III and Edward I when the Barons demanded reform. It was, however, under Edward III that the House of Commons became more powerful as the king became dependent on Parliament for raising taxes.

After World War II ended in 1945, London struggled as a tourist destination. Much of the city had been badly damaged by air raids and the government lacked resources to rebuild the capital. This poster is an early attempt by the British Travel and Holiday Association Board to attract visitors to London. The House of Commons had recently been rebuilt in 1950 after having been totally destroyed during an enemy aircraft bombing attack in May 1941.

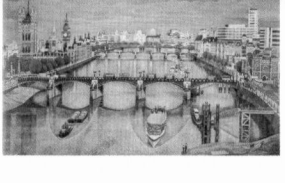

LAMBETH PALACE AND THE HOUSE OF COMMONS.

ACRYLIC PAINTING BY ALFRED DANIELS, RBA, RWS, ARCA, 1978.

Although by the late twentieth century the Thames River had lost its significance as the means by which goods were carried to the city and as the place where ships were built, the river remains the most important and remarkable landmark of London.

Lambeth Palace on the south end of the river, home to the Archbishop of Canterbury since 1200, is the center of the Church of England. The House of Commons, on the left of the river facing east, forms part of the Houses of Parliament (rebuilt in 1852 and anchored by Big Ben) and remains the center of political power for the United Kingdom and Northern Ireland. Lambeth Bridge (built in 1861) is in the foreground and is followed by Westminster Bridge (built in 1750), Hungerford Bridge at Charing Cross (built in 1864), and Waterloo Bridge (built in 1817) in the distance at the bend of the river. Many of the famous buildings that long dominated the City of London are now overshadowed by office and apartment blocks, but can be seen clearly from the Thames because of their proximity to the river.

CURVY MAP OF THE LONDON UNDERGROUND (TUBE) AND DOCKLANDS LIGHT RAILWAY.

ILLUSTRATION BY MAXWELL J. ROBERTS, 2005 (AFTER BECK'S LONDON UNDERGROUND MAPS).

The Underground Service is the central artery that connects the railway and bus services. Today the Tube, as it is known, is the underground network used by most city workers and tourists to get around London, and the long, deep escalators and frequent reminders to "mind the gap" provide fond memories for visitors.

In 1933, Henry Beck's famous schematic of the London Underground was published for the first time. In Beck's map the chaotic tangle of train lines was tamed and converted into simple straightened routes, all easy to see, follow, and understand. Overnight, this powerful image transformed Londoners' perception of the Underground and their city.

Seventy-five years later many more routes have been squeezed into the Underground system, overloading the simple, powerful effect of Beck's work.

On Curvy Map the lines are shown as gentle curves, and changes in direction are smooth; much easier for the eyes to follow than sharp kinks. The result has been described as friendly, fun, and feminine, a map that many people enjoy looking at and that makes them want to travel. The illustrator, who is also a psychology professor, saw Beck's diagram as a challenge for change.